Food in My Kitchen

By Alex Kimathi

Illustrated by Jovan Carl Segura

Library For All Ltd.

Maize flour

Salt

Sugar

Coffee

Milk

Beans

Maize

Mangoes

Tea

Rice

Wheat flour

Eggs

Potatoes

Onions

Tomatoes

Sweet potatoes

Tonight, we will have a feast!

About the contributors

Library For All works with authors and illustrators from around the world to develop diverse, relevant, high-quality books. Visit libraryforall.org for the latest news on writers' workshop events, submission guidelines and other creative opportunities.

Did you enjoy this book?

We have hundreds more expertly curated original stories to choose from.

We work in partnership with authors, educators, cultural advisors, governments and NGOs to bring the joy of reading to people everywhere.

Did you know?

We create global impact in these fields by embracing the United Nations Sustainable Development Goals.

libraryforall.org

You're reading Learner

Learner – Beginner readers

Start your reading journey with short words, big ideas and plenty of pictures.

Level 1 – Rising readers

Raise your reading level with more words, simple sentences and exciting images.

Level 2 – Eager readers

Enjoy your reading time with familiar words, but complex sentences.

Level 3 – Progressing readers

Develop your reading skills with creative stories and some challenging vocabulary.

Level 4 – Fluent readers

Step up your reading skills with playful narratives, new words and fun facts.

Level 5 – Curious readers

Discover your world through science and stories.

Level 6 – Adventurous readers

Explore your world through science and stories.

Edmund Rice
FOUNDATION AUSTRALIA
Liberating Lives Through Education

Original illustrations by Jovan Carl Segura

Food in My Kitchen
Kimathi, Alex
ISBN: 978-1-923339-34-7
SKU04517